ATLANTA-FULTON PUBLIC LIBRARY

D1511370

Editor   Karen Barker
Language Consultant   Betty Root
Natural History Consultant   Dr Gerald Legg

Carolyn Scrace is a graduate of Brighton College of Art in England, specializing in design and illustration. She has worked in animation, advertising, and children's fiction and non-fiction. She is a major contributor to the popular *Worldwise* series and *The X-ray Picture Book* series, particularly **Amazing Animals**, **Your Body**, and **Dinosaurs**.

Betty Root was the Director of the Reading and Language Information Center at the University of Reading in England for over twenty years. She has worked on numerous children's books, both fiction and non-fiction.

Dr Gerald Legg holds a doctorate in zoology from Manchester University in England. His current position is biologist at the Booth Museum of Natural History in Brighton, England.

David Salariya was born in Dundee, Scotland, where he studied illustration and printmaking, concentrating on book design in his post-graduate year. He has designed and created many new series of children's books.

Printed in Belgium.

An SBC Book conceived, edited and designed by
The Salariya Book Company
25 Marlborough Place, Brighton BN1 1UB

First published in Great Britain in 1999 by Franklin Watts

First American edition 2000 by Franklin Watts/Children's Press
A Division of Grolier Publishing
90 Sherman Turnpike
Danbury, CT 06816

Visit Franklin Watts/Children's Press on the Internet at:
http://publishing.grolier.com

Library of Congress Cataloging-in-Publication Data

Scrace, Carolyn.
   The journey of a swallow / written and illustrated by Carolyn Scrace; created & designed by David Salariya.
      p.   cm. --- (Lifecycles)
   Includes index.
   Summary: Describes the life cycle and annual migration of the swallow.
   ISBN 0-531-14519-0 (lib. bdg)
   ISBN 0-531-15418-1 (pbk)
   1. Swallows--Migration--Juvenile literature. [1. Swallows.]
I. Salariya, David. II. Title. III. Series.
QL696.P247S27 1999
598.8'26-DC21   98-30029
                                           CIP

AC

GROLIER
PUBLISHING

©The Salariya Book Company Ltd
MCMXCIX

Printed in Belgium

lifecycles

The Journey of a Swallow

Written and Illustrated by Carolyn Scrace

Created & Designed by David Salariya

W
FRANKLIN WATTS
A Division of Grolier Publishing
NEW YORK • LONDON • HONG KONG • SYDNEY
DANBURY, CONNECTICUT

Swallows are small birds.

In the fall, when the weather is cold, there is less food for them to eat.

Then swallows fly south for thousands of miles (see map on page 26) to find warm weather and food.

In the spring they fly back north again to make a nest and breed.

These long journeys are called *migrations*.

In this book you can follow the amazing migration of a swallow.

Swallows have long
thin wings and large tails.
These help them fly
great distances.
Swallows find their way
by looking at the position
of the sun and the stars
in the sky.

Swallows use the wind
to help them fly.
The moving air lifts and carries
them. This means they do not
have to flap their wings all the time
when they are flying.

It is fall.
Swallows gather in groups.

As the weather gets colder,
the birds start their journey south.

Some swallows fly thousands of miles, from northern Europe to South Africa, or from the northern United States and Canada to Brazil in South America.

Swallows can eat, drink, and even sleep while they are in the air. They eat flying insects by opening their beaks wide and scooping them up.

Some swallows fly over the
Sahara Desert in Africa.

13

The swallows arrive
in the warm south.
Here the air is full of insects.
The birds spend the
winter feeding.

This swallow is flying
low over water
to fill its beak
and drink.

In early February,
swallows start the journey north
to get back home.
Each year they return
to the same place to build a nest.

Swallows like to build their nests in barns or sheds.

17

Swallows use
mud and straw
to build a nest.
They shape the nest
like a cup, and line it
with feathers and hair.

Nests are often built
on a beam or ledge.

The female swallow lays
between 3 and 6 eggs.
Both parents take turns
taking care of the eggs.
They sit on the eggs
to keep them warm.

It takes 2 weeks for the
swallow chicks to grow
inside the egg.

A swallow chick uses its beak
to break open the eggshell.
Both parents catch insects
for their chicks to eat.

The hungry chicks are very noisy.
Their beaks are bright yellow
so that their parents
can see them easily.

In 3 weeks, the chicks
have grown feathers.
Then they are ready
to leave the nest.

In the fall
the young swallows
will start
their own
migration.

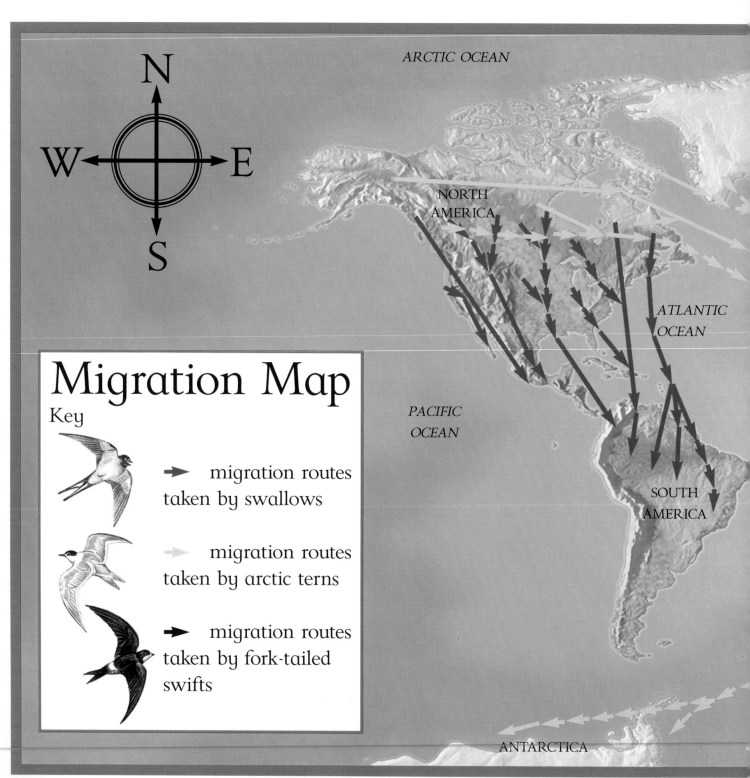

Migration Map

Key

migration routes taken by swallows

migration routes taken by arctic terns

migration routes taken by fork-tailed swifts

ARCTIC OCEAN

NORTH AMERICA

ATLANTIC OCEAN

PACIFIC OCEAN

SOUTH AMERICA

ANTARCTICA

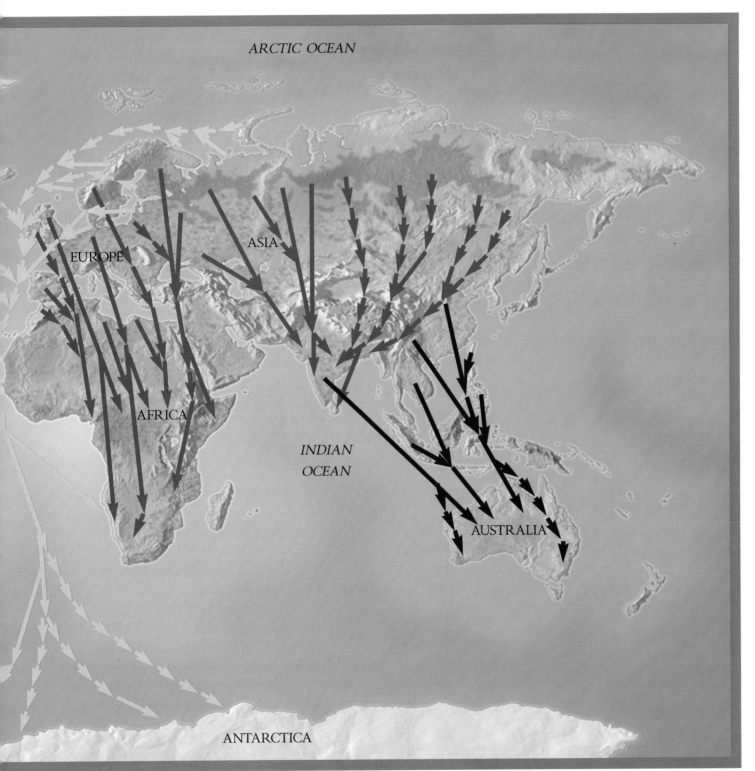

ARCTIC OCEAN

EUROPE

ASIA

AFRICA

INDIAN
OCEAN

AUSTRALIA

ANTARCTICA

27

Swallow Words

Beak
A bird's hard and pointy mouth

Breed
To mate and raise a family

Chick
A baby bird

Egg
Contains the growing chick before it hatches

Feathers
The soft, light coat which helps birds fly. Feathers also keep birds warm and are often colorful

Insect
A small creature with six legs and a body made up of three parts

Migration
The long journey made by some animals to find a warmer place with plenty of food to live for winter

Nest
A hollow place built and used by a bird as a home

Position
The location, or place, where something is. For example, where the sun and stars are in the sky

Shell
The hard covering of an egg. It keeps the chick inside safe

Wings
The parts of a bird's body which it uses to fly

Index

R0091953084

J 598.8 SCRACE   CENTRL
Scrace, Carolyn
The journey of a swallow

CENTRAL LIBRARY
Atlanta-Fulton Public Library